Costume in Context
The Regency

Jennifer Ruby

B.T. Batsford Ltd, London

Foreword

When studying costume it is important to understand the difference between fashion and costume. Fashion tends to predict the future – that is, what people *will* be wearing – and very fashionable clothes are usually worn only by people wealthy enough to afford them. For example, even today, the clothes that appear in fashionable magazines are not the same as those being worn by the majority of people in the street. Costume, on the other hand, represents what people are actually wearing at a given time, which may be quite different from what is termed 'fashionable' for their day.

Each book in this series is built round a fictitious family. By following the various members, sometimes over several generations – and the people with whom they come into contact – you will be able to see the major fashion developments of the period and compare the clothing and lifestyles of people from all walks of life. You will meet servants, soldiers, street-sellers and beggars as well as the very wealthy, and you will see how their different clothing reflects their particular occupations and circumstances.

Major social changes are mentioned in each period and you will see how clothing is adapted as people's needs and attitudes change. The date list will help you to understand more fully how historical events affect the clothes that people wear.

Many of the drawings in these books have been taken from contemporary paintings. During the course of your work perhaps you could visit some museums and art galleries yourself in order to learn more about the costumes of the period you are studying from the artists who painted at that time.

Acknowledgments

The sources for the drawings have, in some cases, been contemporary paintings and drawings. In particular: Introduction: miner, after George Walker, peasant woman, after William Johnston White; page 27, after William Johnston White; pages 32, 38, 39, after G. Cruickshank; pages 34, 35, after J. Townsend and G. Cruickshank.

Typeset by Tek-Art Ltd, Kent
and printed and bound in Great Britain
by The Bath Press, Bath
for the publishers
B.T. Batsford Ltd
4 Fitzhardinge Street
London W1H 0AH

ISBN 0 7134 5992 1

Contents

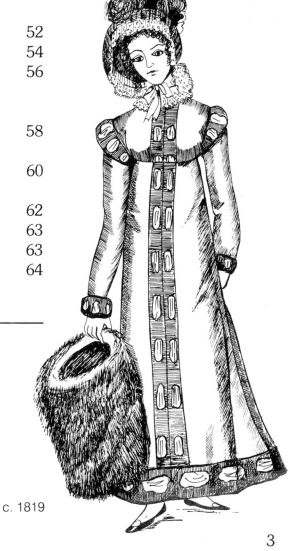
c. 1819

Date List

1800	George III is king but is suffering increasingly from bouts of madness. England is at war with France. The 'Classical' look is fashionable for women and clothes are simple and unrestricting, echoing the message of 'freedom' from the French Revolution. Men are wearing coats, waistcoats and breeches, though pantaloons are becoming popular.
1805	Battle of Trafalgar. Nelson is fatally wounded.
1808	Heathcote invents a bobbin net machine which introduces a cheaper alternative to hand-made lace.
1811	The Prince of Wales is created Prince Regent. Along with Beau Brummell, he leads male fashion favouring elegant smooth lines and an impeccable fit in clothes. The Luddite Riots.
1814	Scott's Waverley novels are begun.
1815-23	Shelley, Keats and Byron are writing.
1815	Battle of Waterloo. Napoleon is defeated. The restoration of the French Monarchy. Women's clothes become more romantic. Architect John Nash is engaged by the Prince Regent to transform and extend Brighton Pavilion which is to become a favourite haunt of the Prince. As a result, Brighton becomes a centre of fashion.
1816	Beau Brummell falls from favour. The frock coat makes its appearance. Men are wearing trousers more and more.
1820	Death of George III. The Prince Regent becomes King. The Romantic movement is in full swing.
1821	Sir Walter Scott's novel *Kenilworth* is published. A revival of interest in Tudor fashions and a vogue for Scottish tartans.
1824	The waistline is gradually resuming its normal position, corsets and tight lacing follow. Skirts are becoming wider.
1825	The first public railway is opened.
1829	The first omnibus in London, introduced by Shillibeer. The Metropolitan Police Force is established. The sleeves on women's dresses are becoming even larger.
1830	Death of George IV. William IV comes to the throne.
1835	Over 100,000 power looms are weaving cotton materials in Britain.
1836	Sleeves collapse, bright colours give way to greens and browns. Men's clothes are becoming much more conservative.
1837	Death of William IV, Victoria becomes Queen.

Introduction

Historically, the period covered by this book (1800-1837) was a very exciting one. The French Revolution of 1789 was an explosion that shook the Western world and during the opening years of the nineteenth century, England was in the grip of war with France. The Agricultural and Industrial Revolutions that had begun in the eighteenth century were now making more of an impact on everyday life as technological changes made for greater efficiency and an increased number of products. Transport and communications were improving all the time. The canal network was used extensively for transporting products and raw materials, there were many more stage- and mail-coaches, in 1825 the first public railway opened and there was increased circulation of books, newspapers and periodicals. It was also a fruitful period in the arts. Painters like John Constable and Joseph Turner, poets like William Wordsworth and Samuel Taylor Coleridge and novelists like Jane Austen and Sir Walter Scott were all creating great works of art which are still loved and admired today. All these events were, of course, reflected in the fashions of the time.

During the first two decades of the nineteenth century, women's fashions followed the vogue for neo-classicism. The stiff, elaborate styles and heavy materials of the eighteenth century gave way to simplicity and flimsiness. Dresses were plain and high-waisted and hair was worn short and tousled, or in long ringlets in the style of the ancient Greeks. Muslin was the most popular material and some women even dampened their skirts to make the material cling seductively to their bodies – quite an unsuitable practice in the English climate!

c. 1834

After 1815, and the restoration of the French Monarchy, fashion became more romantic. Flounces, frills and ribbons, puffed and slashed sleeves were added to previously plain dresses and hemlines rose slightly. Soft muslins began to be replaced by stiff cottons, silks and satins.

In 1820 the waistline began to drop, reaching its natural level by 1827. Corsets and tight lacing became fashionable and hats, sleeves and skirts became progressively wider. The Romantic movement was in full swing and the Romantic woman looked rather like a butterfly with her tiny waist and enormous sleeves and skirts. She was also supposed to be 'sensitive' and of a delicate constitution, and indeed, she probably felt so beneath her tight stays!

In 1836 these flamboyant fashions began to fade. The enormous sleeves collapsed, skirts became slightly longer and bright colours gave way to greens and browns at the beginning of Victoria's reign.

Men's fashions became increasingly conservative during this period. The emphasis was on superb fit and impeccable cut rather than on extravagant design, and the waistcoat was the only garment which was allowed more colour and pattern. The development of this style is generally attributed to George Bryan Brummell who was one of the most famous dandies of modern times. For a while he was quite a favourite of the Prince Regent who was also a lover of fashion and of pleasure. The Prince spent many thousands of pounds both on his wardrobe and his leisure pursuits and was continually surrounded by wealthy young men eager to follow the latest trends in fashion.

The main development in men's dress was in the introduction of new garments. Late in the eighteenth century knee breeches were being replaced by calf or ankle length pantaloons, which were in turn gradually superseded by trousers. (At first trousers were almost indistinguishable from pantaloons which is why the Americans call trousers 'pants', the shortened version of 'pantaloons'.) Both the frock coat, with its distinctive front edges, and the top hat made their appearance at this time, and were to become popular garments for the rest of the century. Fine white linen shirts with fancy cravats were a status symbol worn throughout the period.

There were also a number of technical innovations in the textile industry at this time. Research and experimentation resulted in a new range of mineral dyes and an increase in brilliantly coloured synthetic dyes. Factory machines were continuously improving, which meant increased production of wool, linen, cotton, silk and lace which were then made up by tailors and dressmakers who had to cope with the ever changing styles. The invention of the tape measure early in the century enabled tailors to obtain more accurate body measurements when constructing the popular tight-fitting clothes!

Miner
c. 1814

All these changes hardly affected the poorer classes, however, who could rarely afford to follow fashion. Their clothes were usually home made from plain, coarse materials – or second-hand and therefore out of date. It is ironic that these were often the very people who were slaving in factories and workshops under dreadful conditions in order to produce the fashions worn by the rich. For many of Britain's poor, life was harsh. While some worked for 16 hours a day in the factories, others found themselves out of work as machines were gradually replacing craftsmen. This, together with the effects of the Napoleonic wars, caused widespread unemployment and misery which sometimes lead to rioting.

Even the middle classes were not always fashionably dressed. It often took some time for London fashions to reach the provinces which meant that those who were not moving in fashionable circles were often a little out of date with their clothes. Many middle class women made garments for themselves or tried to update old ones. Sometimes a maidservant would help with the sewing – as happens in some of Jane Austen's novels.

In this book you will meet a wealthy family and see their changing fashions over the years. In addition, you will see other people from very different backgrounds so that you can compare and contrast the clothes they wear. This will give you a picture of what it was like to live and work many years ago during the first part of the nineteenth century.

c. 1818

A Rich Landowner, c. 1805

This is Lord Thomas who owns a large country estate in the south of England, where he lives with his family and servants. He is very wealthy and is always dressed in fashionable clothes.

Here he is wearing a single-breasted blue riding coat with gilt buttons, a striped waistcoat, long breeches, top boots and a muslin cravat. Sometimes instead of knee breeches, Lord Thomas might wear pantaloons, which are tight fitting and reach to his ankle, or trousers which are just becoming fashionable. On the right you can see him wearing trousers while relaxing in his study. They are quite tight and have a short side slit above the ankle.

He is also pictured in his evening attire which consists of a double-breasted coat with a straight front waist, breeches, white stockings and black slippers. Under his arm he carries his 'chapeau-bras' which is a crescent-shaped opera hat which can be folded and carried.

You can also see some of his underwear and his favourite watch which came from France.

Lord Thomas wears his hair 'à la Titus' which means short and tousled after the Roman Emperor of that name. He is clean shaven except for side whiskers and he likes to wear a little rouge or walnut juice on his cheeks.

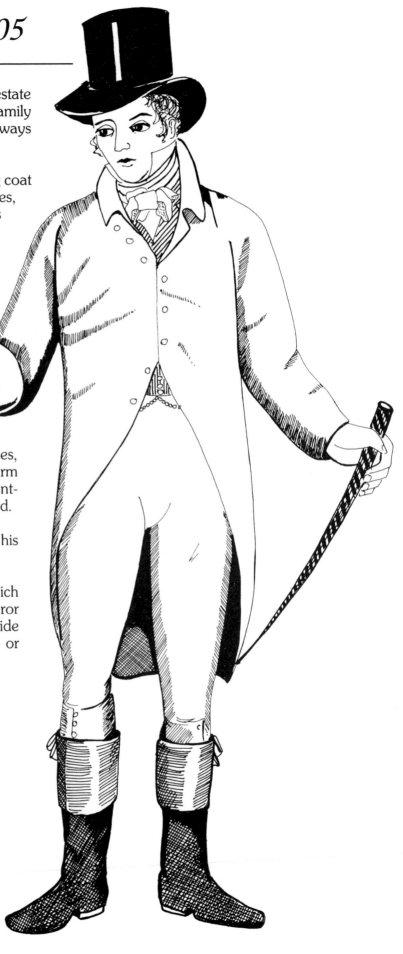

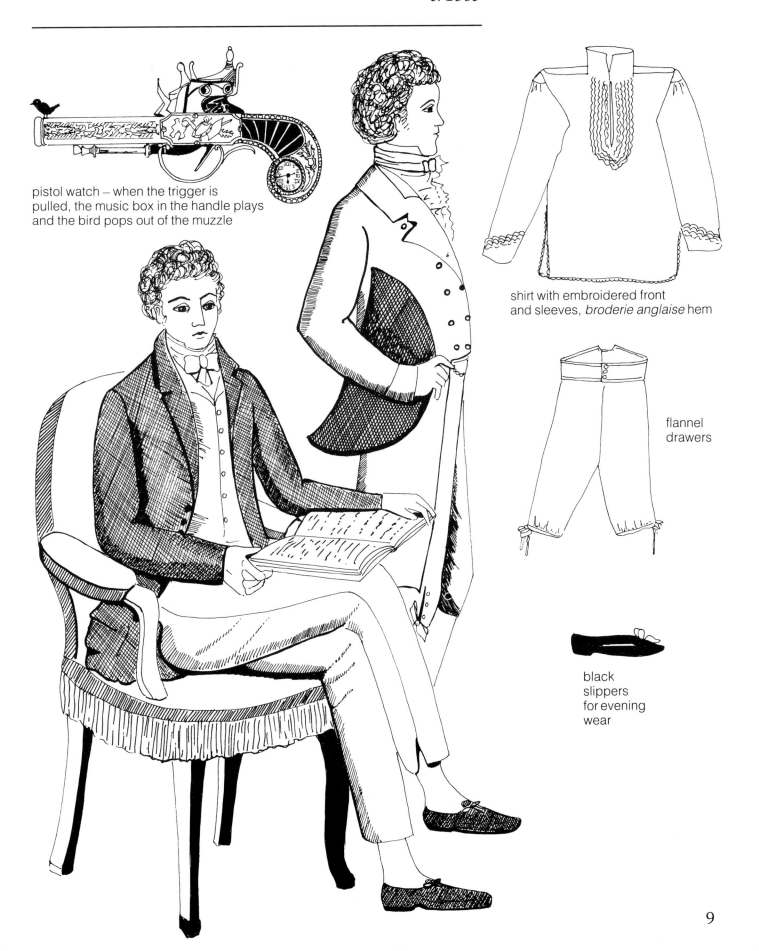

pistol watch – when the trigger is
pulled, the music box in the handle plays
and the bird pops out of the muzzle

shirt with embroidered front
and sleeves, *broderie anglaise* hem

flannel
drawers

black
slippers
for evening
wear

The Landowner's Wife, c. 1806

At the beginning of the nineteenth century the 'Classical' look was fashionable for women. This meant that the emphasis was on simple lines and soft draping fabrics after the manner of the ancient Greeks. Muslin and cambric were popular materials and dresses were often thin enough to expose the shape of the body. Hair was worn either long in Grecian curls or short and tousled à la Titus.

This is Eleanor, Lord Thomas's wife. She has an extensive wardrobe and on this page you can see her wearing one of her evening gowns which is made of fine muslin. It is high waisted with a square neckline and the skirt is trained. She is also wearing long white gloves and black satin slippers. Her hair is arranged in curls.

Other items from her wardrobe are pictured opposite. They include a pelisse which is an outdoor coat and two day dresses, both of which are high waisted and have simple, elegant lines.

Eleanor owns many hats. She usually wears a mob cap in the daytime and in the evening she might exchange this for a turban. Poke hats are very fashionable. When she is wearing one of these her face is completely hidden by the brim.

A very important accessory at this time was the reticule, which was a small handbag used to carry a handkerchief or money. Reticules became popular because the old style of pocket, which ladies used to wear under their dresses and over their petticoats, were no longer appropriate as they would have spoiled the line of the new straight dresses. Other accessories included muffs, gloves, fans and parasols.

Eleanor likes to wear rouge on her cheeks and sometimes she wears false bosoms made of wax or cotton. These were quite popular. A contemporary poet wrote:

"My Delia's heart I find so hard, I would she were forgotten.
For how can hearts be adamant when all the breast is – cotton?"
(*The Oracle* 1800)

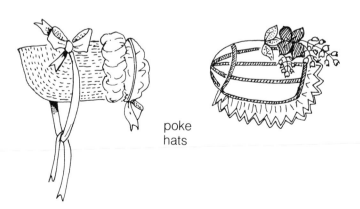

poke
hats

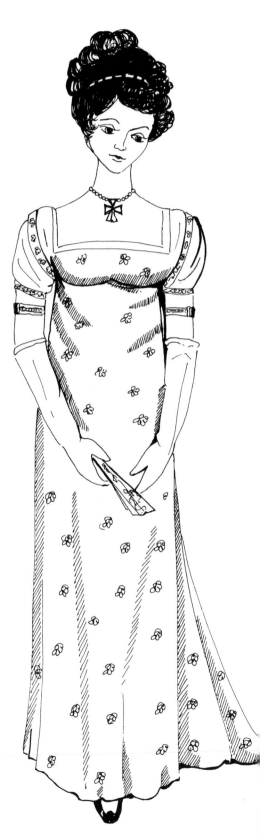

silk
mob cap
trimmed
with ribbon

rear view of
hairstyle

pelisse

day
dress

white satin
muff with coloured
embroidery

white satin
reticule

white tulle collar

corset with
elastic webbing
side inserts

11

A Soldier, c. 1808

This is Robert, Lord Thomas's younger brother who is an officer in the First Foot Guards. He is wearing a bicorne hat decorated with a plume, a red coat with gold buttons, white pantaloons, hessian boots and a red sash around his middle.

During the first few years of the nineteenth century England was at war with France. Many young men like Robert were involved in the fighting serving under the Duke of Wellington. See if you can find out more about some of the battles and the types of uniform that were worn.

On the far right, Robert is pictured out of uniform. If you compare his two outfits you will see how fashionable morning and walking dress has adopted some of the elements of military wear. He is wearing a double-breasted riding coat with curved fronts, a muslin cravat, a short waistcoat, light coloured breeches and hessian boots. He is carrying his leather gloves and has seals hanging from his waist.

Men's coat collars were rather large at this time and in order to make the collar easier to turn down, a large 'M'-shaped notch was often cut into the material at the point where the collar met the lapel. You can see this on Robert's coat.

The fashion for elegant simplicity and superb cut in men's clothing is usually attributed to George Bryan Brummell, better known as 'Beau' Brummell. He was one of the most famous dandies of all time and he strove for perfection of cut and fit in his clothes, which were made from fine, plain materials. He prided himself that his clothes did not show a single wrinkle and that his breeches fitted like skin. The style aimed at unobtrusive perfection and it was copied by many fashionable young men of the time. The only extravagance was in neckwear and cravat tying was considered to be an art. Beau Brummell's valet was quite used to spending hours helping his master to arrange his to perfection.

Children's Fashions, c. 1810

Here is Lady Eleanor with her youngest children, Charles, aged six, Edward who is four and two-year-old Harriet. It is the custom to dress little boys as girls until they are four or five years old. Consequently, Edward is wearing a low-necked frock with short cotton trousers showing beneath.

Charles is wearing a skeleton suit which is a very popular outfit for small boys. It consists of a tight-fitting jacket and trousers which are buttoned on above the waist. (Charles Dickens wrote, in *Sketches from Boz*, that these suits gave young boys the appearance of having their 'legs hooked on under their armpits'!) Harriet is wearing a muslin cap and a high-waisted muslin frock.

Eleanor's oldest children are both away at boarding schools. Catherine is 13 and quite a young lady; she likes wearing the latest fashions. Here she is wearing a pelisse of sarcenet which is trimmed with Egyptian crepe and antique lace. Her gloves and slippers are made from matching kid and she has a reticule of painted velvet. Her hair is parted in the middle and arranged in fashionably dishevelled curls.

Philip is 12 and is boarding at Eton. He is wearing a short tail coat, a waistcoat, pantaloons and hessian boots. Around his neck he wears a muslin cravat and he is carrying his leather gloves.

Find out all you can about boarding schools in the nineteenth century.

Two Servants, c. 1810

Lord Thomas has many servants who wait on him and his family and help to keep the house and estate in good working order.

The huge kitchen has a roasting range and two large ovens. Ellen is one of the cooks and she is busy preparing a meal for the family. She is wearing a mob cap decorated with ribbon, a cotton print dress and a white apron.

At present, Ellen is not very busy. However, there are occasions when Lord Thomas has many guests staying at the mansion. At these times the kitchen is a constant hive of activity as elaborate menus are prepared. See if you can find out what kind of food might be served at a large banquet.

John is a footman. One of his jobs is to help serve food at the dining table. He is wearing the livery given to him by Lord Thomas. It consists of a double-breasted tail coat with curved fronts and a high collar, breeches, silk stockings, black shoes and a cravat. He is also wearing a queue wig which is rather old fashioned but is customary for footmen who must at all times appear immaculate. In fact, footmen continued to wear wigs well on into the nineteenth century and when these were finally discarded they resorted to powdering their hair instead!

John does not always wear his livery because his jobs are many and varied. For example, when he is cleaning the knives or silverwear he wears an overall, a leather apron and a white apron on top of that.

A Housemaid, c. 1810

This is Mary, who is a housemaid. She works long hours and has a lot of lifting, cleaning, fetching and carrying to do. She gets up very early in the morning with the other maids to clean the fireplaces and after this job is done she puts on a clean apron to make the beds.

Here she is wearing a mob cap, a high-waisted cotton print dress, flat slippers and a white apron. Although she does not have much money, Mary likes to be fashionable. She and the other housemaids watch Lady Eleanor and try to copy her clothes.

One of Mary's evening duties is to fill the warming pans with hot coals and place them into the beds of the Duke and his family. Find out more about what it would be like to be a serving maid at the beginning of the nineteenth century.

A Gardener, c. 1810

This is Mary's sweetheart, William, who works in the garden helping to keep the flower beds tidy and the lawns neat and trim.

He is wearing a fashionable square-cut tail coat, a waistcoat and hard-wearing leather breeches. His ankle boots are called highlows and are very popular among workmen. He is also wearing a cocked hat, a neck scarf and an apron.

William and Mary are planning to get married. After they do, they will both continue to work on Lord Thomas's estate.

A Farm Labourer and his Family, c. 1810

Lord Thomas owns many acres of land in the surrounding area which are farmed by a few tenant farmers. John's brother Harry is a farm labourer on one of these farms. It is now harvest time and there is a great deal of work to do.

Harry is wearing a felt hat, a short coat and waistcoat, knee breeches, leather gaiters and stout boots. His coat is made of corduroy. This material was a great boon to workers at this time because of its strength and durability.

Harry's wife Molly usually helps in the fields at harvest time in order to earn a little extra money. However, this year she is doing less work because she has a young baby to care for.

Molly is wearing a bedgown which is a very popular garment among working women. It is a kind of three-quarter-length jacket with long sleeves and a cross-over front, (although it is sometimes fastened with tabs), and she is wearing it over her skirt and petticoat. She also has on a white apron, a mob cap trimmed with ribbon and a neckerchief.

Little Jane, who is four years old, is wearing a patched linen dress under a white pinafore and baby Hal is wearing only a cotton vest.

As Harry and Molly do not have a great deal of money, Molly makes quite a few clothes for herself and the children. Besides needlework, she knits garments for Jane and Hal and the woollen clothes help to keep them warm in their drafty cottage during the winter.

Harry and Molly also try and contribute a penny a week to the clothing club that is run by the local parson's wife. This money builds up week by week so that they can buy second-hand clothes for their best or 'Sunday' outfits.

The couple consider themselves very lucky as Harry has a permanent job and they have a roof over their heads. For many others life is much harder. At harvest time extra workers are taken on to help and some of them are very poor indeed. Often they only possess one outfit of clothes and if this gets soaking wet in the rain they have to go to bed while trying to dry out their garments, frequently putting them on again the next day while they are still damp.

Over the page you can see Farmer Westlake, Harry's boss, talking to some of the harvest workers who have paused for lunch.

Harvest Time, c. 1810

Farmer Westlake is wearing an embroidered smock over his clothes to protect them but the rest of the workers are wearing their ordinary garments. The women have on sleeveless bodices and unmatching skirts, mob caps, bonnets and aprons. The older man is wearing a jacket, waistcoat, breeches, woollen stockings and boots.

Choose one of the characters from this picture and write a full description of his or her clothing. What would their garments be made of and what colours would they be? What kind of lifestyle would the farm worker have?

23

Three Sailors, c. 1810

Harry's younger brother George is a sailor. He ran away to sea when he was only eleven years old and served as a cabin boy on Nelson's ship the Victory. He can tell exciting tales about the famous battle of Trafalgar.

Now he has been promoted to an ordinary seaman. He has no regular uniform but he generally wears a jacket, trousers, shirt and a waistcoat. He also wears a black hat and a scarf around his neck.

On the opposite page you can see Dick, the cabin boy and Ben, the ship's carpenter. Dick is wearing a coat, shirt and waistcoat with a white apron over his breeches. He is very young and works hard, cleaning the officers' quarters and acting as a general servant.

Ben is wearing two waistcoats over his striped shirt, trousers, a neck scarf and a scarf turban-fashion, around his head. He has a pot of hot pitch to caulk any leaky seams on the ship.

It is interesting that trousers were worn by sailors long before they became fashionable for civilians. English sailors were wearing them as early as 1737 though they did not catch on in fashionable circles until early in the nineteenth century.

In 1810 sailors' trousers were gradually becoming wider in the leg and by 1817 they were referred to as 'gun mouthed'. This was a reference to the swelling of a gun muzzle and equivalent to the later 'bell-bottom' trousers.

Find out more about some of the famous sea battles of the early nineteenth century. What was life like aboard ship? What kind of food did the sailors eat and what kind of punishments did they receive? What were the press gangs?

Rich and Poor, c. 1812

It is now 1812 and we will return to Lord Thomas's family.

Catherine is now home from school. While out walking she sees Molly and her daughter who have been to market. Seeing their patched, worn clothes, Catherine feels quite ashamed when she thinks of all the fine dresses, bonnets and shoes that she possesses and she resolves to give some of her garments to the parson's wife for the clothing club that she runs.

In this picture Catherine is wearing a spencer, which is a short-waisted, long-sleeved jacket. It is decorated with lace. Underneath she is wearing a muslin walking dress. Her hat is trimmed with ribbons and flowers.

Below are some of her other bonnets and two of her shoes.

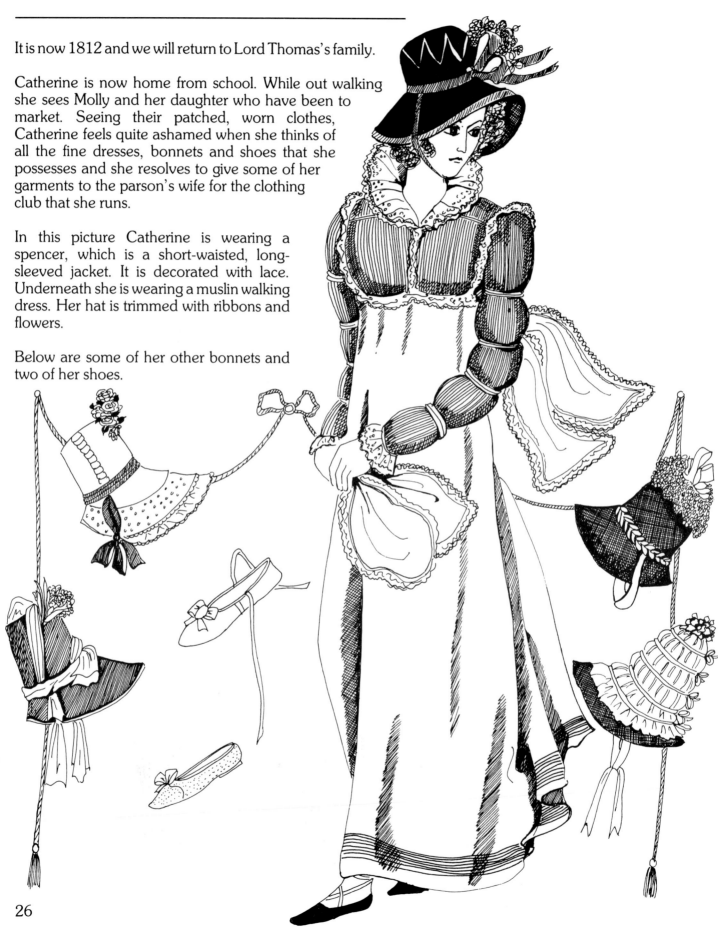

Molly is wearing a straw hat over a mob cap, a shawl over her long-sleeved patched linen dress and a white apron. She is carrying a poultry basket and is using her apron as an extra container.

Jane is wearing a bonnet, a neckerchief and an unmatching cotton bodice and skirt.

Imagine some of the other people who would have been at the market. Draw a picture of a group of them talking together at a market stall. What would they be wearing?

It is now 1816 and Lady Eleanor and her two eldest children are visiting her brother and his family who live in Brighton. Brighton has become a very fashionable place to visit as it is frequented by the Prince Regent, so Lady Eleanor and Catherine are eager to take a look at the latest styles in dress during their stay.

A more romantic look is now fashionable for women. Dresses are adorned with frills and lace and neck ruffs are popular. Lady Eleanor (left) is wearing a white muslin dress embroidered with small blue and red flowers. It has a high waist and the neckline and long sleeves are ornamented with ruches. She wears a neck ruff, a white muslin cap and flat slippers.

Catherine has on a white lawn dress edged with flounces, a high neck ruff, tartan ribbon sashes, flat shoes with crossover straps and a hat 'à la Pamela'.

Some ladies at this time took to wearing bustles shaped like sausage rolls which they tied under the top of their skirts in order to create the fashionable 'Grecian bend'. Sometimes these ladies looked a little extreme and were ridiculed by cartoonists of the day.

Philip is now a young man of 18 and he also likes to wear the latest fashions. He is wearing a double-breasted coat with M-notch lapels, and flapped pockets, a cravat, pantaloons, hessian boots and he is carrying his top hat and gloves.

caricature of the 'Grecian bend'

A Dandy, c. 1816

Here is Philip's Uncle Randolph, who is quite a dandy. He mixes in all the fashionable circles in Brighton and can always be seen in the latest styles.

Here he is wearing an early form of frock coat, a garment which was to become very popular during the reign of Queen Victoria. Underneath this he is wearing a shirt, waistcoat and cossacks which are voluminous trousers pleated into a waistband and drawn in at the ankles. He also has on a cravat, boots and a small flat hat. (This type of hat was only briefly a fashion among dandies.)

On the right you can see Randolph in his dressing room. His toilet takes as long as any lady's! As it is fashionable for men to have pinched-in waists, many gentlemen spend some time squeezing themselves into tight-laced corsets. (The Prince Regent rather liked this fashion, and in 1814 Henry Brougham remarked, in a letter to Creevey: 'Prinnie is in a bad way. They have positively ordered him to give up his stays as the wearing of them any longer would be too great a sacrifice to ornament – in other words, would kill him . . .'.)

Randolph's valet is busy lacing up the stays which must be very uncomfortable and not very healthy! Randolph is also wearing a shirt and cravat, trousers and boots. His valet is not so fashionably dressed. He has on a shirt and cravat, a jacket, breeches, stockings with clocks and shoes.

Like many men, Randolph wears a little make-up in the form of rouge. What other toiletries does he use? See if you can find out more about some of the cosmetics used by men and women in the early nineteenth century. Were any of them harmful?

What would be the effects of wearing such a tight-fitting corset every day?

Randolph is getting ready to go out. Where is he going? Find out all you can about sports and pastimes in the nineteenth century.

MORNING
AMUSEMENTS

Wrestling~

Monkeys
~
Dancing
Dogs

QUADRILLE
DANCE

A Parson and his Wife, c. 1821

It is now 1821 and there is great excitement on and around Lord Thomas's estate as it is time for the Michaelmas celebrations. Each year Lord Thomas opens the grounds of his estate for one day for games, dancing, feasting and merrymaking. All the local people attend, dressing up in their finery and joining in the fun.

Here is the parson and his wife who are on their way to the celebrations. The parson's clothes are a little old-fashioned, befitting his profession. He is wearing an overcoat over his coat, waistcoat and breeches, woollen stockings, a flat hat and shoes with buckles. His wife has on a poke bonnet which completely hides her face, a muslin dress embroidered with small flowers and decorated with a flounce at the hem, and she carries a reticule which she made herself. It is made of cream velvet with hand-painted flowers and piped with silk cord. (Painting on velvet was a popular pastime at this time.)

London dresses, c. 1802

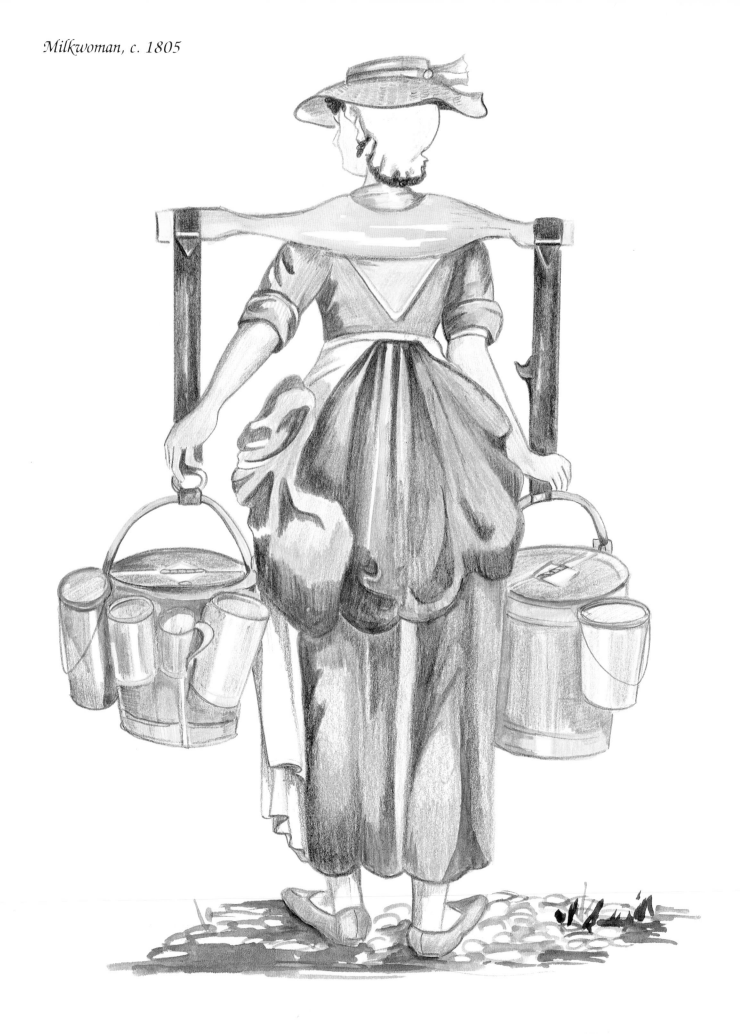

Milkwoman, c. 1805

Lampman, c. 1805

Men's fashion, c. 1810

Ball dress, 1810

Summer dress, 1827

Printed cotton dress, 1828

Seaside costumes, 1825

Morning and evening dress, 1831

A Farmer and his Wife, c. 1821

Farmer Westlake and his wife are also on their way to join in the fun. Mr Westlake is wearing a bowler-shaped hat, a morning coat with an M-notch in the lapel, breeches, stockings and shoes tied with bows. His wife is wearing a dress with straight long sleeves trimmed with bands of gathered muslin bows, a poke bonnet and a double pelerine with lace edging. She is carrying her reticule.

Celebrations, c. 1821

Here you can see everyone enjoying themselves on Lord Thomas's estate. All kinds of activities are taking place and refreshments have been provided. Everyone is dressed in their best clothes, even if they do not have a great deal of money. The publication of Sir Water Scott's novel *Kenilworth* has generated an interest in Tudor fashion – neck ruffs and puffed and slashed sleeves are fashionable.

Trousers are becoming more popular with men and are often worn in preference to breeches. The children are dressed quite comfortably with the boys in skeleton suits and the girls in soft muslin dresses. Molly and her youngest daughter are here selling fruit. What are they wearing? Can you find a lady in a riding habit?

Evening Wear, c. 1821

Lord and Lady Thomas have invited many of their friends and family to a banquet and dance at the mansion as part of the celebrations.

Catherine is now married and she and her husband have travelled from their home in London to attend the banquet.

Catherine's husband, Herbert Welbourne, is a wealthy banker and also an MP. He is wearing a blue dress coat with gilt buttons and a velvet collar, a waistcoat, a white shirt and a silk cravat and flesh coloured breeches. He is also wearing silk stockings with clocks and flat shoes. He is carrying his chapeau bras.

Catherine is wearing a beautiful embroidered cream coloured ball gown with satin trimmings and puffed sleeves, long white gloves and her curled hair is decorated with ostrich feathers.

Also pictured opposite are two different kinds of hairstyles that are popular for evening wear, and flat evening slippers, which most of the ladies are wearing for the dancing.

c. 1821

hair arranged in an Apollo knot with pearl diadem and long pins (1824)

elaborately decorated turban

slippers, tied with long strings, wound around the ankle

37

The Quadrille, c. 1821

The quadrille is a dance for four couples and was very popular during the early nineteenth century. Here are some of Lord Thomas's guests enjoying themselves performing it.

The men are wearing slim-fitting dress coats, cravats, breeches or pantaloons, silk stockings and flat pumps.

The women are wearing low-necked dresses with puffed sleeves and decorated hems, long white gloves, flat slippers and are carrying fans. (The waistline on women's dresses has now dropped slightly although it will not resume its natural level until about 1824.) Their hair is arranged in curls and is decorated with combs and feathers.

The lady on the right is wearing a bustle under her skirt giving her the 'Grecian bend' shape.

It is interesting that the fashion in men's clothing, with the pinched-in waists and padded chests, gives them a slightly feminine look. Some men even wear padding at their chests to accentuate their tightly laced waists and also wear perfume and carry scented handkerchiefs.

Ladies' Fashions, c. 1826

Ladies' fashions have now moved away from the straight, classical lines that were previously popular and the new look is a more romantic one. The waist has resumed its normal position, shoulders are wider and often padded and are balanced by fuller skirts. Hats are becoming much larger. Women of all classes are squeezing themselves into tightly laced corsets, sometimes damaging their health. (One tradesman wrote in 1828 that his daughters: 'are unable to stand, sit or walk as women used to do. To expect one of them to stoop would be absurd. My daughter Margaret made the experiment the other day: her stays gave way with a tremendous explosion and down she fell and I thought she had been snapped in two.')

There is still an interest in Tudor fashion and Marie Stuart caps and neck frills are fashionable.

Here is Catherine at her London home. She is wearing a dress which has wide shoulders and is decorated with ruches and steel buttons. Her large hat is trimmed with a tulle veil and ribbons and she is carrying an embroidered handkerchief. On the opposite page you can see the underwear that she wears underneath the dress in order to give it this shape.

In the large picture opposite, Catherine is wearing a pelisse of green satin with a double pelerine and large pearl buttons down the front. The pelisse has a chinchilla border and she is carrying a matching muff.

You can also see a few other items from her extensive wardrobe.

Why do you think it was harmful to wear very tightly-laced corsets all day?

hair with side curls, 'Marie Stuart' cap of fine muslin, matching neck ruff

white cotton cap

down filled cotton sleeve puffs

chemise with short sleeves

bustle

white lawn petticoat

white cotton pocket

underwear

gloves

white silk reticule with silk embroidered flowers and leaves

kid heelless shoes

A Wealthy Banker, c. 1826

Here is Catherine's husband, Herbert. As he is very wealthy he is always dressed in the latest fashions whilst in London.

Here he is wearing a silk top hat, a piqué waistcoat, a cloth coat with a velvet collar and silk buttons, and light-coloured trousers fastened under the ankle. Around his neck he is wearing an eyeglass on a chain and he is carrying a cane with a ribbon twisted around it.

On the opposite page you can see other items from his wardrobe. These include one of his greatcoats which he wears over his suit on cold days, and two of his many cravats.

At this time small waists were as important to men as they were to women and in order to emphasize his, Herbert is wearing very tight stays. Dressing elegantly is very important to him. During one week he uses 20 shirts, 24 pocket handkerchiefs, 30 cravats and 12 waistcoats! The reason he requires so many clothes is because he is always changing. For example, he might breakfast in a dressing gown, change to go to the bank or to Parliament, change again for afternoon tea, once more for dinner and then finally to go to bed! Fortunately, he has people to wash his clothes for him.

Herbert also owns a large house in the country. When Parliament is not in session he often takes the family there. On these occasions he wears more informal clothes for his favourite pursuits of riding and shooting.

shirt

double-breasted
greatcoat

cloth
gaiters

handkerchief

embroidered
tobacco pouch
and white clay
pipe

cravats

Children's Clothes, c. 1826

Here is Catherine with her three children, Edmund, who is six, five-year-old Rosamund and Miranda who is just two.

As legs were strictly 'taboo' in the nineteenth century, from about 1803 when little girls' dresses were worn above the ankle, they began to wear cotton trousers under their skirts instead of petticoats. These were worn partly to add extra warmth, but also to provide a little modesty for active little girls in flimsy blow-away skirts!

Edmund and Rosamund are playing in the garden. Rosamund has on a flimsy dress with a low neckline and short sleeves, which is decorated with lace and flowers. Her pantalettes are made of cotton and have a lace trimming. Her hair has been plaited and the two plaits have been coiled up and pinned on each side of her head. She is also wearing flowers in her hair.

Edmund is wearing wide, comfortable trousers, a cotton blouse with a broad collar, and a short jacket.

How practical do you think these clothes are for playing in?

A Policeman, c. 1829

Now we will move outside on to the busy streets of London and meet some other people who lead lives very different to those of Catherine and her family.

The Metropolitan Police Force was set up in 1829 and it was felt that there would be great advantage in having a uniform so that policemen would be instantly recognized in the streets.

Colonel Rowan was one of the two joint Commissioners who originally headed the Force and he felt that the uniform should be 'quiet' as he did not want his men to resemble soldiers. The outfit that was chosen was a blue coat, blue or white trousers, according to the season, and a tall black hat which was reinforced with cane strips and a leather top. A white letter and number were embroidered on to the stand-up collar of the coat. The letter indicated the policeman's division and the number was his own identity.

Ralph is a constable and he enjoys his job, parading the streets of London keeping law and order. He is wearing his official uniform. In the winter he is issued with a dark brown overcoat and he also receives two pairs of boots annually.

Scotland Yard have one of these original uniforms in their museum. See if you can find out more about the British Police Force. How successful were they in the early nineteenth century in their fight against crime?

A Letter-Carrier, c. 1829

In 1772 the Post Office appointed a large number of letter-carriers to make free house-to-house deliveries. They were given official uniforms in 1793.

Gilbert is a letter-carrier and he is wearing a red cut-away coat with a blue collar, a black top hat with a gold band and cockade, and a grey waistcoat and trousers.

As well as delivering letters, Gilbert also receives them from people who have not had time to hand them in to the Post Office.

He is rather like a walking pillar box, parading the streets late in the afternoon before the night mail coaches depart. He rings a bell to announce his presence and customers hand him their letters which go into his mail bag. (This practice was discontinued in 1846 and in 1852 the first pillar boxes were set up.)

What do you think it would have been like to be a letter-carrier? How different would the job have been to that of today's postmen?

A Dustman, c. 1829

Round another corner we meet Dusty, the parish dustman. Dusty travels around the streets with his cart ringing a bell and crying 'Dust-ho!' People put their rubbish into boxes, tubs or baskets and set it outside their homes for him to collect.

He is wearing a brown coat, a blue waistcoat, red breeches, striped blue and white stockings, a checked blue shirt, brown gaiters and hob-nail boots. He has a red cap on under his fan-tail hat which has a padded neck flap for protection when he is carrying heavy dust baskets. His gaiters prevent ash from going down into his boots.

Dusty is a very colourful character. Draw a picture of him in his costume with his horse and cart.

The two boys on the opposite page are apprenticed to a chimney sweep. They travel with him on his rounds and climb up the chimneys to remove the soot.

Two Climbing Boys, c. 1829

Jack (left) is wearing an old smock over patched trousers and Tom has on a jacket, shirt and ragged breeches. Both boys are wearing caps which have metal plates on the front of which is engraved their master's name and address. Tom is carrying a hand brush and a scraper and Jack is holding a hand brush and carrying an extendible sweep's brush. (This was invented in 1802.)

The life of climbing boys was very hard indeed. Many were sold to master sweeps either by their parents who were too poor to keep them, or by the parish authorities if they were orphans. Some were beaten and had pins stuck into their feet to make them climb up the dark sooty chimneys. At first their knees, elbows and heels bled all the time but gradually they became accustomed to the work and their skin hardened, although their life remained a terrible one of poverty and hardship.

William Blake (1757-1827) wrote a poem about the plight of climbing boys. Look up 'The Chimney Sweep' and find out more about the cruelty imposed upon these children.

A Milkmaid, c. 1829

This is Sarah who is a milkmaid. She is wearing stays over a white shift, a blue apron, a short skirt, a top hat and boots. Sarah carries her milk pails suspended from a wooden yoke across her shoulders.

In London the retailing of milk in the streets started at the beginning of the eighteenth century. Girls like Sarah would roam the streets calling 'Milk below!' or 'Mio'. Sometimes they actually milked the cows themselves very early in the morning for there were several farms in the London suburbs. For example, there were farms at Paddington, Knightsbridge and Tottenham Court Road though this seems hard for us to imagine now!

In 1864 milk was brought into London by train for the first time and the whole trade was then organized on a larger scale. Milk went from depots and was delivered to houses by roundsmen who had their own particular form of dress. See if you can discover what these roundsmen would have worn.

On the right you can see Sarah's mother, Hannah with her two youngest children, Kate and Tom. Hannah is wearing a mob cap, a woollen shawl and a white cotton apron over a patched linen dress.

Kate is wearing a cotton pinafore over her dress and Tom has on an old patched dress that used to belong to his sisters. Both children wear cotton caps.

A Cottage Interior, c. 1829

Compare the clothes worn by Hannah and her children with those of Molly and her children (p. 21). Nearly 20 years have passed yet the clothes of poorer people have not changed very much. Would there be any advantages or disadvantages to living in London rather than in the country?

A House Party, c. 1831

It is now 1831 and we will return to Catherine and her family who are spending two months at their country mansion in the south of England. Herbert has decided to have a house party and he and Catherine have invited some of their family and friends to stay for a week.

On the left you can see Charles, one of Catherine's brothers, and his wife Cecily who have travelled from London for the occasion. Charles is wearing a knee-length frock coat of dark cloth, a striped cravat, light-coloured trousers and square-toed shoes. His waistcoat is embroidered and has narrow lapels and he is carrying his hat and cane. He has quite long side whiskers, as this is now fashionable.

Cecily is wearing a striped silk dress with Donna Maria sleeves, white gloves, a ruff collar and a silk bonnet trimmed with ribbon. She is carrying a handkerchief.

Charles and Cecily have brought many clothes with them so that they can change for all the varied activities that they will take part in, such as walking, riding, dining and dancing. On this page you can see some of the garments they have brought with them.

The sleeves on ladies' dresses have become wider than ever, as have the very full skirts. However this width is always balanced by a tiny waist, so Cecily never goes anywhere without several corsets. The cotton dress on the right will be suitable when she goes walking or perhaps for afternoon tea.

One of Charles's dress suits is also pictured here. He might wear this for dinner or dancing in the evening.

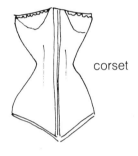

corset

colour-printed cotton dress

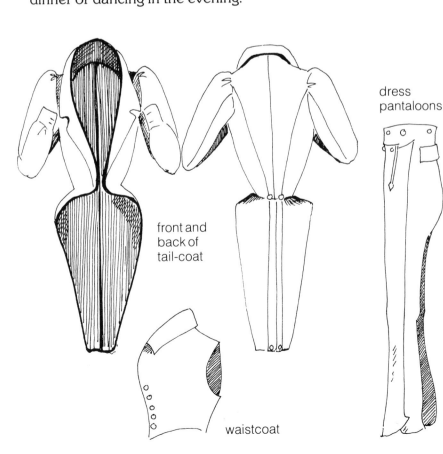

front and back of tail-coat

waistcoat

dress pantaloons

Sports Wear, c. 1831

All the family enjoy hunting, shooting and riding and of course they have different outfits for each of these pursuits.

On the opposite page Catherine's brother Edward (left) is wearing a hunting costume, which consists of a red coat with gilt buttons, white breeches, top boots and a black top hat. His brother Philip is wearing his shooting outfit, which consists of a dark blue coat with gilt buttons, breast flapped pockets and large 'hare' pockets inside the skirts. He is also wearing tight buff strapped trousers, a top hat and gloves.

Harriet, Catherine's sister, is now 23 years old. She particularly enjoys riding and for this she is wearing a tight-fitting jacket with a velvet collar and very wide sleeves, a full skirt, riding boots and a top hat with a gauze veil. Some items of her attire are borrowed from the male fashions. Which are these? Why do you think that women might like a slightly more masculine look when out riding?

Walking, Dining, Dancing, c. 1831

Catherine and Herbert's guests have quite a busy week with all their different activities. When they are not riding, hunting or shooting they might go for walks around the beautiful gardens or further afield on the estate. Here you can see Harriet out walking in the garden. She is wearing a white dress of jaconet printed with blue flowers. It has a broad collar trailing over three-quarter-length balloon sleeves with a velvet ribbon at the neck. She is also wearing a trimmed shawl around her shoulders, blue gloves and a ribbon decoration in her hair.

In the evenings there is a great deal of dining and dancing. On the opposite page, Charles's wife Cecily and Edward's wife Constance are dressed in evening wear. Cecily (left) is wearing a dinner dress which has gauze sleeves over short, puffed sleeves, a cross-over front and a tiny waist. Her hat is made of dark crepe and is decorated with ostrich feathers.

Constance is wearing a ball dress of white satin gauze with wide sleeves and a skirt trimmed with a deep flounce of lace and bouquets of flowers. She has flowers decorating her hair and long white gloves.

Both the men and women would require many changes of clothing for a week like this. How many times a day might they change?

Two Weddings, c. 1835

It is now 1835 and Harriet is getting married to Richard, the son of a rich neighbour of her father's. Their wedding is a very grand affair with many guests and after the ceremony there will be a wedding breakfast at Harriet's home. Harriet is wearing a dress of blonde lace over white satin and a blonde lace veil. Richard is wearing a black coat and pantaloons, and a gold-trimmed chestunut coloured cashmere waistcoat.

Meanwhile, is Scotland, a very different ceremony is taking place.

Sarah the milkmaid has eloped with Jonathan, the son of a rich solicitor. His family do not approve of their marriage so they have run away to Gretna Green where marriage ceremonies are frequently conducted by the ferryman, the blacksmith or the toll keeper. Here you can see them at the blacksmith's premises. Sarah is wearing a white dress, a red cloak with a fur cape and a feather trimmed bonnet. Jonathan is wearing a long blue cloak, a top hat, a brown coat and white trousers. The blacksmith is in his shirtsleeves, waistcoat, breeches, gaiters and shoes. He also has on his leather apron and a black round cap.

Conclusion, c. 1836

Now we come to the end of our period and the eve of the long reign of Queen Victoria, which began in 1837.

Here is Harriet and her husband, who are out walking. Harriet is wearing a green, black and white tartan dress with a tightly fitting bodice, a full skirt and a white linen collar. The fashion for extremely large sleeves has suddenly diminished and Harriet's are moderately wide at the top, tapering in to narrow wrists. She is also wearing a tie-on bonnet with a flower spray and she is holding her parasol and a small embroidered purse.

Richard is wearing a frock coat, a light waistcoat with a roll collar, a black cravat and dark woollen trousers. His black top hat is made of silk and he is wearing white gloves and holding his cane.

In the background you can see Dan, a seller of Staffordshire pottery who travels by canal to London to sell his wares. He is wearing a shabby top hat and scarf and a long smock. Obviously Dan is from a very different background to Harriet and Richard.

Compare the fashions of 1836 with those worn by Harriet's parents in 1805. What are the differences? Did the clothes of poor people change as much?

During the course of this book we have seen people from all walks of life. How do their clothes reflect their different lifestyles and occupations? Do you think clothes still reveal as much about a person today?

Glossary

bedgown	a lady's cross-over gown of three-quarter length, usually made of cotton and worn by working women (*page 21*)
bicorne	a man's hat (*page 12*)
chapeau-bras	a crescent-shaped opera hat which could be folded flat (*pages 9, 36*)
clock	a pattern worked in silk on the side of a stocking (*pages 31, 36*)
cockade	a rosette worn in a hat as a badge of office or as part of livery (*page 47*)
cossacks	voluminous trousers pleated into the waistband and drawn in at the ankles; they became popular after the visit of the Tzar to London in 1814 (*page 30*)
dandy	a person dedicated to smartness (*pages 30, 31*)
Donna Maria sleeves	full to the elbow and then tight to the wrist (*page 52*)
fan-tail hat	a working man's hat with a long neck-flap to protect the neck and shoulders (*page 48*)
frock coat	a man's skirted coat with straight front edges (*pages 30, 52, 61*)
gaiters	a covering of stiff fabric or leather for wearing below the knee as protection against the wet and mud (*pages 20, 22, 43, 48*)
Grecian bend	a fashionable look which was created by wearing a bustle high under the skirt at the back (*pages 29, 39*)
hare pockets	pockets large enough to put a hare into when out shooting (*page 54*)
hessian boot	knee-length boot with heart-shaped peak at the front and often decorated with a tassle at the centre (*pages 12, 13, 15, 29*)
highlows	leather ankle boots worn by workmen (*page 19*)
jaconet	thin cotton, between muslin and cambric (*page 56*)
livery	a uniform provided by wealthy persons for their servants (*page 17*)
M-notch lapel	an M-shaped opening at the join of a man's coat collar and lapel (*pages 9, 13, 29, 33*)
mob cap	a woman's cap with puffed out crown and deep frilled border (*pages 16, 27, 51*)
Pamela bonnet	a straw bonnet with a tall crown and ribbons tied under the chin (*page 28*)
pantalettes	long ruffled drawers worn by little girls under their dresses (*pages 44, 45*)
pantaloons	very tight-fitting men's leg-wear usually made of stretchy fabric or soft leather (*pages 12, 15, 29, 38*)
pelisse	a woman's coat usually made along the same lines as the frock (*pages 11, 14, 15*)
piqué	a stout, ribbed cotton fabric (*page 42*)
poke hat	a lady's hat with a large brim extending over her face (*pages 10, 32, 33*)
queue wig	a wig with a lock of hair tied or knotted at the back (*page 17*)
reticule	a small handbag used to carry a handkerchief, money etc. (*pages 11, 15, 32, 33, 41*)
sarcenet	a thin silk textile, plain or twilled (*page 15*)
skeleton suit	a small boy's suit consisting of a tight jacket and trousers buttoned on above the waist (*pages 14, 34, 35*)
slashing	cutting slits of varying length into a garment for decoration (*page 35*)
spencer	a short-waisted, long-sleeved lady's jacket (*page 26*)
Titus, à la	a term applied to hair worn short and tousled in the style of the Roman Emperor of that name (*pages 9, 12*)
top boots	men's boots reaching to just below the knees; they had wide, turn-over tops of a light shade and loops on each side for pulling on (*page 8, 54*)
tulle	fine silk net used for veils and dresses (*pages 11, 40*)

Book List

Barthorp, Michael	*British Infantry Uniforms Since 1660*, Blandford Press, 1982
Black, J.A. & Garland, M.	*A History of Fashion*, 2nd ed., Orbis Publishing, 1980
Bradfield, Nancy	*Costume in Detail, 1730-1930*, Harrap, 1968
Bradfield, Nancy	*Historical Costumes of England 1066-1956*, Harrap, 1958
Brook, Iris	*English Costume of the 19th Century*, Black, 1929
Braun-Ronsdorf, Margarete	*The Wheel of Fashion*, Thames & Hudson, 1964
Byrde, Penelope	*A Frivolous Distinction: Fashion and Needlework in the Works of Jane Austen*, Bath City Council, 1979